# CAMBRIDGE PRIMARY LANGUAGE

STUDY SKILLS   LEVEL 4   CHARLES CUFF

## Contents

# The problem of wildlife conservation

**1** Before you read pages 3 and 4 write one or two things you already know about wildlife conservation.

**2** **Read** the first paragraph on page 3 **carefully.** Write a sentence to explain what it tells you.

**3** The word 'habitat' is used twice on page 3. Read the second paragraph and write what you think 'habitat' means. Use a dictionary to check your explanation.

**4** **Search** pages 3 and 4 to help you write
   **a** a list of at least eight things which wild animals are killed for;
   **b** at least four ways in which people spoil the habitats of wild animals.

**5** Why is wildlife destroyed when hedges are cut down or when marshes are drained?

**6** Two reasons for killing animals are given in the last paragraph on page 4. Do you agree that animals should be killed for these reasons? Write a few sentences to explain your thoughts.

**7** Choose one of the animals drawn on pages 3 or 4. Use books to help you write a short report about it. Try to write some information under each of these **headings:**
**its size and appearance**
**its natural habitat**
**why it is in danger**

*Study plan*

**1** Find the book (or books).
**2** Find the information.
**3** Write notes as you read the information.
**4** Close the book (or books).
**5** Use the notes to help you write the report in your own words.

Wild animals face many dangers. For example, some are eaten by other animals and others die of thirst or hunger. The greatest dangers for wild animals, however, are often caused by people.

black buck

tiger

Many types of wild animal have become extinct, or been put in danger of extinction, because of the activities of people. In some parts of the world, farming has made the land unfit for animals. Hedges have been cut down to make larger fields. These hedges were the **habitat** of a great many plants and animals. Too much fishing and hunting has robbed the seas of wildlife—the blue whale is one animal that has suffered. Huge areas of rain forest are being cut down and marshes are drained. The wildlife in these areas is destroyed. As farms and cities and traffic have grown, the air, land and water have become polluted. Natural **habitats** have been upset and animals have died.

# The problem of wildlife conservation

| white pelican | turtle | panda | bison |

Wild animals are killed for many reasons. Types of kangaroo have disappeared because large numbers of them were killed and their meat sold as pet food. Animals with fur are threatened because their fur is used for clothes. Other animals are hunted because their skins are made into luxury items such as expensive shoes and cases. Whales are killed for meat and oil. Some animals are killed so that perfumes can be made from parts of their bodies. Elephants face extinction because of their valuable ivory tusks and rhinoceroses are in danger because their horns are used as a medicine. Rare birds are captured to sell as pets and they often die in their unnatural captivity.

Some people believe that there are good reasons why some wild animals have to be killed. They say that without the whaling industry, thousands of whalers and other workers would lose their jobs. Others claim that the numbers of seals must be kept down because they eat fish which is needed to feed people. Clearly there are no easy solutions to wildlife conservation.

# Whales (notes)

**Read this carefully**

Whales are hunted and killed.
Their bodies are cut up on special ships
and used for many purposes.
There is a danger that more species
of whale will soon become extinct.

**Now do this**

Below are some **notes**. Use the notes to help
you write some paragraphs of information
about whales. Start by writing a good title
for your information.

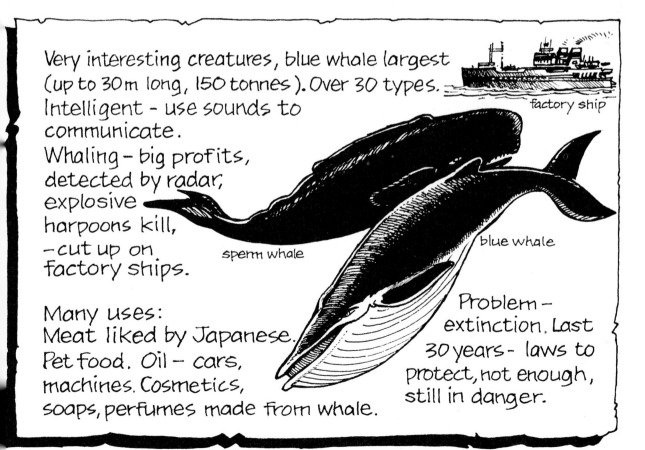

Very interesting creatures, blue whale largest
(up to 30m long, 150 tonnes). Over 30 types.
Intelligent - use sounds to
communicate.
Whaling - big profits,
detected by radar,
explosive
harpoons kill,
- cut up on
factory ships.

factory ship

Many uses:
Meat liked by Japanese.
Pet food. Oil - cars,
machines. Cosmetics,
soaps, perfumes made from whale.

sperm whale

blue whale

Problem -
extinction. Last
30 years - laws to
protect, not enough,
still in danger.

# Sorting living things

## Read this information carefully

All living things can be sorted into two main groups – animals and plants. Animals themselves can also be sorted into two groups – animals with backbones and animals without backbones. The animals in each of these two groups can then be sorted into smaller groups. For example, the animals with backbones can be put into five groups:
fish, amphibians, reptiles, birds and mammals.

1. Use the information and the drawings to help you complete a chart like this
   Use a whole sheet of paper and space your chart out well.

2. Write **notes** about the information.

3. Use your **notes** to help you write a paragraph about sorting living things. Close this book while you are writing the paragraph.

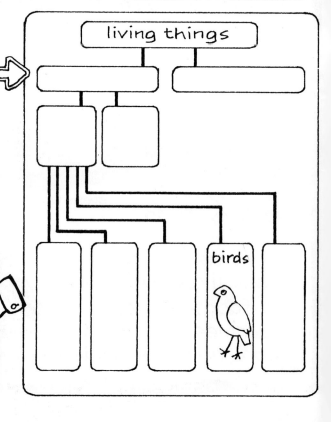

When you write notes, write important words only. Leave out short words like **it the and**

HANDY HINT

# The energy problem

**1** **Read** the first paragraph on page 8 **carefully**. Pick out the four main ways it says people have obtained energy. Write a list of them.

**2** Read the second paragraph on page 8 carefully and write a few sentences to explain what the energy problem is.

**3** Talk with a partner about some of the changes there might be in your lives if fossil fuels ran out tomorrow. Make a list of some of the possible changes.

**4** **Search** pages 8 and 9 to help you write
    **a** a list of five sorts of energy which will not get used up;
    **b** two modern ways of getting energy which are like methods used in the past.

**5** Write some **notes** about two ways you could help save fuel (electricity, gas, oil, petrol) at home, at school and when travelling.
Set your notes out like this

Saving fuel
1. At home
   a
   b
2. At school
   a
   b
3. When travelling
   a
   b

HANDY HINT
This is an outline.
The numbers, letters and headings help you to set down your notes in order.

# The energy problem

### The use of energy

Our ancient ancestors used their own bodies to do work.
Later animals were used to do work. Then people built
windmills and mills with waterwheels. These used the
natural energy of wind and flowing water to turn
machinery. Today huge amounts of coal, gas and oil are
used to provide the energy we need. The energy is
needed for lighting and heating and to power machines
and vehicles.

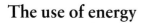

### The problem

Coal, gas and oil have taken millions of years to form
underground. They are made from the decayed remains of
plants and animals and are called **fossil fuels**.
If we keep using these fuels in such great amounts
they will run out. Some experts believe that they will
disappear in your lifetime. Then there would have to
be great changes in everyday life.

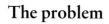

### Solving the problem

People are trying to solve the energy problem.
Solar panels are used to capture light from the Sun.
The natural heat below the Earth's surface is
being used. People have designed highly efficient
windmills and built dams which use the energy of
wind and moving water to produce power to do work.
Some countries use nuclear energy although many
people fear its dangers. All these sorts of energy
will not run out.

### What can I do?

While scientists are searching for new ways of obtaining
energy, you must try not to waste the energy we have.
You can do this at home, at school and when travelling.
One way would be to copy your ancestors and make more
use of your muscles!

# The pollution problem

## Do this first

Before you read page 11
**a** write one or two things you already know about pollution;
**b** describe any sorts of pollution you have noticed yourself.

## Now do these

**1** **Read** each section of page 11 **carefully** and for each section write one sentence to explain what it is about.

HANDY HINT
Put your five sentences together so that they make a paragraph about the pollution problem.

**2** Write what you think are the two most important sentences on page 11.

**3** **a** How do you think water is sometimes polluted?
**b** How do you think air is sometimes polluted?
**c** How do you think soil is sometimes ruined?
(See page 13 for help.)

**4** What connection is there between the pollution problem and the problem of wildlife conservation? (See pages 3 and 4.)

**5** Write about ways you might be able to help solve the pollution problem:
**a** now
**b** when you are an adult.

1 We live on the surface of a planet called Earth. We depend upon its **air, water and soil**. If we destroy these things we shall destroy ourselves and all life on Earth. This is exactly what people will do if they are not more careful.

2 **Without air**, living things quickly die. Breathing clean air is vital to good health. In spite of this, air has sometimes been polluted with dangerous chemicals and materials. These have caused illness and death.

3 **Without water** to drink, human beings can only survive for about three days. Yet this life-supporting liquid has often been polluted. It has been made poisonous to people, animals and plants.

4 **Without soil**, plants and animals could not exist. The soil is only a thin layer on our planet and it has taken millions of years to form. Unfortunately people have often changed the soil so that many things will not grow in it. It is then washed away or blown away.

5 **Pollution** is a serious problem, but there is some hope. The danger has been noticed. Many people are working for a safe and clean Earth. Perhaps you can help.

# The pollution problem

The sentences and drawings on page 13 are about pollution of **air, water** and **soil**. They need to be sorted.

**1** Set them out in a better way. Start with **air** like this:

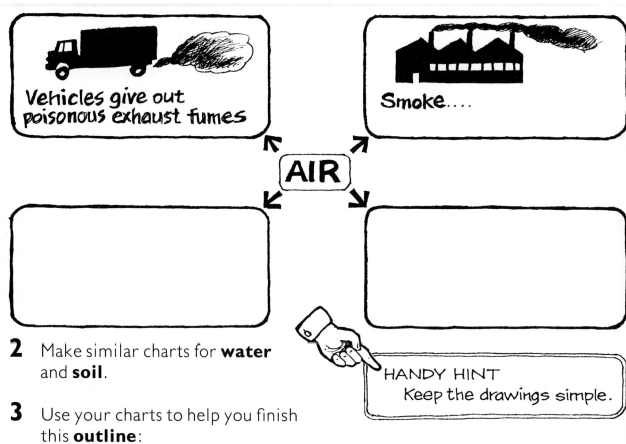

Vehicles give out poisonous exhaust fumes

Smoke....

AIR

**2** Make similar charts for **water** and **soil**.

HANDY HINT
Keep the drawings simple.

**3** Use your charts to help you finish this **outline**:

   1 **AIR** can be polluted by:
     a            c
     b            d

   2 **WATER** can be polluted by:
     a            c
     b            d

   3 Little will grow on **SOIL** if:
     a            c
     b            d

HANDY HINT
An **outline** with numbers, letters and headings helps you set down ideas in order. Make an **outline** to help you when you have to write a report.

Smoke from chimneys dirties the air.

Forests have been cut down and not replanted.

Sewage is pumped into the sea.

Some soil has been over-farmed and no goodness put back.

Nuclear radiation makes the atmosphere dangerous.

Fertilisers and weedkillers are washed into rivers.

Too much animal grazing has ruined vegetation.

Dangerous dust escapes and is harmful to lungs.

Oil leaks from tankers.

Land is cleared by burning but then it is difficult for farmers to grow plants for some time.

Detergents and chemicals pollute rivers.

Vehicles give out poisonous exhaust fumes.

# Town map

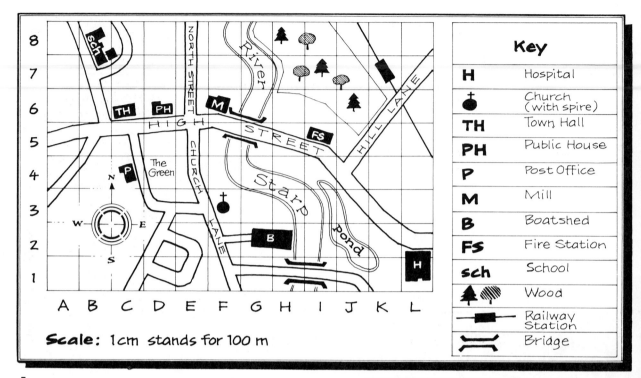

**Scale:** 1cm stands for 100 m

**Key**

| | |
|---|---|
| **H** | Hospital |
| ✝ | Church (with spire) |
| **TH** | Town Hall |
| **PH** | Public House |
| **P** | Post Office |
| **M** | Mill |
| **B** | Boatshed |
| **FS** | Fire Station |
| **sch** | School |
| 🌲🌳 | Wood |
| —▭— | Railway Station |
| ⤳ | Bridge |

**1** Name a building which is
  **a** north east of The Green,
  **b** north west of The Green,
  **c** south east of The Green.

| Building | Grid square |
|---|---|
| | |
| | |
| | |
| | |

**2** Choose any four buildings in the village and write their names and grid squares.

**3** Use a ruler and the scale to help you write
  **a** the length of the pond;
  **b** the straight line distances between
    (i) the two bridges,
    (ii) the school and the church.

**4** What is the distance in metres by road from
  **a** the Post Office to the Railway Station?
  **b** the Boatshed to the Mill?
  **c** the Town Hall to the Hospital?

**WORK LIKE THIS :**

1 Bend a piece of string to the shape of the road.
2 Straighten the string.
3 Measure it in centimetres.
4 Use the scale to find the distance in metres.

# Pie charts

**Pie charts**
This is a **pie chart**.
It shows what Lisa did during
24 hours. Each division stands
for approximately one hour.

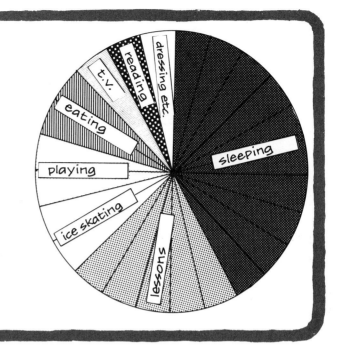

**1** How many hours did Lisa spend
   **a** sleeping?
   **b** doing school work?
   **c** watching TV?

**2** Make a pie chart to show how you
usually spend Saturday or Sunday.
Make each one-hour division
fifteen degrees (15°).
(You will need a protractor.)

**3** Use your pie chart to help you
write a list of the main things
that you do during that day.
Start with the thing that takes
most hours.

**4** Make a pie chart to show the birth
months of 18 children you know.
Let each division of 20° stand
for one person.

**5** In which month were most of the
children born?

**6** List any months in which none of
the children were born.

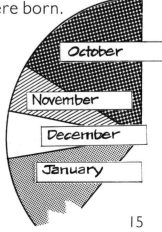

# Using an encyclopedia

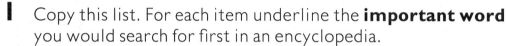

This encyclopedia has 20 volumes.
The information is in **alphabetical order**.

**1**  Copy this list. For each item underline the **important word**
you would search for first in an encyclopedia.
  **a**  blue whales
  **b**  printing in modern times
  **c**  tyres made of rubber
  **d**  Roman chariots
  **e**  the barn owl
  **f**  types of soil

**2**  After each item in the list write which volume on page 17
you would search first for information about it.

Encyclopedias often have **guide words**
to help you. The word on the left is
the first subject on page 128.
The word on the right is the last
subject on page 129.

**3**  Write out the list below.
After each item write
**on pages 128 and 129**
or **before pages 128 and 129**
or **after pages 128 and 129**
to show whereabouts the subject
would be if it was in the
encyclopedia shown on page 17.

python  pump
printing  puppet
pygmy

**4**  Search a real encyclopedia for the
items listed in **1**.
Make a chart to show where you
found the information.

| subject | encyclopedia | volume | pages |
|---------|--------------|--------|-------|
| blue whales | | | |

HANDY HINT
Don't forget to
use the guide words.

## Read this first

Encyclopedias often have an **index**.
The index tells you the exact pages on which to find information.
Here is part of one entry:

> **Trees**  **18**–230a;  deciduous trees **18**–234b;
> evergreen trees **18**–235a;  yew trees **19**–147b;
> It shows

```
              ┌─────── the volume where the information is
18–230a  └─ the page where the information is
     ┗─────── the column where the information is
```

(*Note*: a → first column, b → second column)

**1** Copy this chart and use the information above to help you complete it.

| | VOLUME | PAGE | COLUMN |
|---|---|---|---|
| Tree information starts | | | |
| Evergreen trees | | | |
| Yew trees | | | |

**2** **Search** an encyclopedia to help you **write or draw** an answer for each of the questions opposite. Make a chart to show where you found the information for each answer.

**a** When was Elizabeth I Queen of England?
**b** What is the height of Mount Everest?
**c** How deep is the Pacific Ocean?
**d** What is unusual about the head of Janus?
**e** What does a manatee look like?
**f** What does the Chinese flag look like?

FOOTNOTE
> Use an index if there is one.

# Wheels and axles

For some of these activities you will need to **read** the paragraphs on page 19 and 20 carefully. For other activities it will be better to **search** the pages.

**1** Write a good **heading** for each of the paragraphs about wheels and axles.

**2** **a** How do you think tyres improved wheels?
**b** How do you think spokes improved wheels?

A **fact** is something true – often it can be proved.
An **opinion** is what a person thinks – it might be right or wrong.

**3** Write whether each of these statements is **fact** or **opinion**. Give a reason for each choice.
**a** Wheels and axles are the most important inventions.
**b** Spokes have been used to improve wheels.
**c** Rolling logs gave people the idea of a wheel.
**d** The Sumerians made wheels from shaped planks.

**4** Choose six steps in the development of the wheel and axle. Draw a picture for each of the steps. Write a sentence for each picture. Start like this

1 Perhaps a log gave people the idea of a wheel.
2
3
4

**5** **Look carefully** at things we use to help you draw
**a** something which has wheels with spokes;
**b** something which has wheels with cogs;
**c** something which has wheels joined by belts or chains.

HANDY HINT
Make a rough copy first.

Wheels and axles are simple things and there are so many around us that we hardly notice them. However, the wheel and axle are among the most important inventions. Many modern machines and vehicles depend upon them.

Possibly nature gave our ancestors the idea of making wheels. Perhaps a girl or boy kicked a log so that it rolled. Maybe someone rolled a round stone down a slope. Anyway our ancestors discovered that logs could be used as rollers under heavy objects. By using rollers the heavy objects could be moved more easily. Of course, it would have been hard to roll the logs over rough ground and each log would not stay under the object for very long.

Maybe one day an unknown inventor cut slices off a log and made the first wheels. Perhaps he or she fixed a much thinner log to the base of a rough sledge. This log would have been the axle. Holes were probably made in the wheels so that they could be fitted on the axle. A peg would be needed to keep the wheel on the axle.

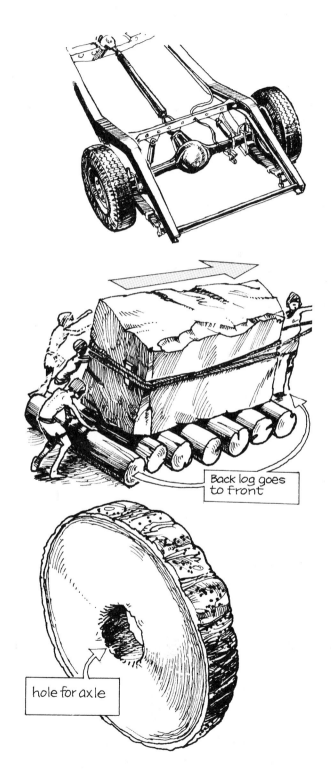

Back log goes to front

hole for axle

# Wheels and axles

The next improvement came when a wheel was built from shaped planks of wood fixed together. You can see a wheel made like this in a picture which is about 5000 years old. The picture was found at the ancient city of Ur (in modern Iraq) where the Sumerians lived.

Since those far-off times there have been many more improvements and changes to wheels and axles. Tyres of leather, metal and rubber have been used. Wheels with spokes took the place of heavy solid wheels. Cog wheels are used in many sorts of machinery and so are wheels which are linked by belts or chains.

*Printing press driven by solar energy [1882]*

wheel

flywheel

belt

pulley wheel

spoked wheel

cogwheels

# Printing

For some activities you will need to **read** paragraphs on pages 22 and 23 carefully. For other activities it will be better to **search** the pages.

**1**   **a**   Why did the monks have to write more and more books?
     **b**   What often happens when there is a great problem like the monks being unable to write enough books?

**2**   How old was Gutenberg when he died?

**3**   How do we know Gutenberg printed well?

**4**   What do you think was the most important thing Caxton did? Write whether your answer is a **fact** or your **opinion**.

**5**   Write two sentences from the information about printing which you think are **very important**. Then write two sentences which are **not so important** and which could have been left out. Write reasons for your choices.

**6**   Read the first paragraph about printing. Close this book and write one sentence to explain what the paragraph tells us. Choose another paragraph and do the same.

**7**   Make a **flow chart** to explain the way Gutenberg printed. Start like this

HANDY HINT
Write notes –
not full sentences.

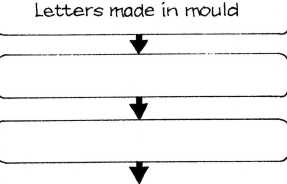

Letters made in mould

21

# Printing

## An important invention

Printing is a very important invention. It is important to everyone who has ever read a comic, a paper or a book. It was the first way of spreading news, ideas and knowledge to huge numbers of people.

## Handwritten books

The first manuscripts or books were written by hand. In Europe monks usually did this task. As more and more people learned to read, the monks could not write all the books that people wanted.

## Gutenberg's printing press

Often when there is a problem someone discovers a solution. As far as we know Johann Gutenberg, who lived from 1400 to 1468, invented a way of printing in about 1440.
Letters were made in moulds. These letters could be set out to make a page of words. The letters of each page were then covered with ink. Paper was put on the printing press. It was pressed onto the inked letters so that the words were printed onto the paper. This could be done many times over. Many copies of a book could be printed. The individual letters could then be moved and used to make a different book.

### The first printed Bible

Gutenberg's printing was very good.
His masterpiece, the first printed
version of the Bible, still exists.
It was printed in about 1455 and
is called the Gutenberg Bible.
It is a very beautiful book.

### The Caxton Press

An English merchant called William Caxton lived in Belgium.
In about 1475 he bought a printing press and used it to
print the first book in the English language. He returned
to England soon afterwards and set up a printing press
near Westminster Abbey in London. Caxton printed about a
hundred different books before he died.

### Modern presses

Printing presses have improved a great deal since the times
of Gutenberg and Caxton. Many presses are now computerised
so that they can produce the enormous numbers of books which
are read in the modern world.

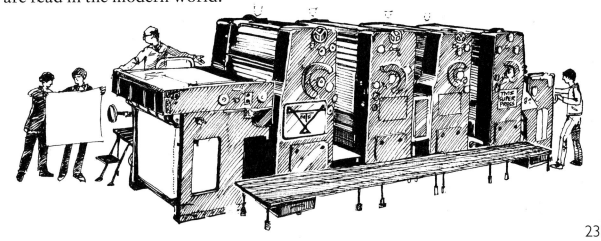

# Edison and the light bulb

For some of these activities you will need to **read** paragraphs on pages 25 and 26 carefully. For other activities it will be better to **search** the pages.

**Remember!**
Write important words only.

**1 a** Write **notes** about the first paragraph.
 **b** Use your notes to help you rewrite the paragraph in your own words. Close this book while you are writing the paragraph.

**2 a** Write **notes** about the second paragraph.
 **b** Use your notes to help you answer these questions without reading the paragraph again:
  (i) In what way was Edison like other inventors?
  (ii) How long did Edison take to invent his light bulb?
  (iii) Which three scientists had carried out experiments which helped Edison?
 **c** Now use the information on page 25 to help you check your answers. Mark them yourself.

**3** Use the diagram of the light bulb on page 26 to help you write a short paragraph to describe the bulb.

**4** Why doesn't the thin wire inside a light bulb burn away?

**5** Do you agree that bulbs and tubes will improve even more? Write a reason for your opinion.

**6** Write six words which would describe Edison. For example

clever, hard-working

**7** Write a conversation which Swan and Edison might have had to end their arguments. Start like this:

**Edison:** We must stop arguing. I'm sure we can solve our problems....

High on the list of the world's important inventors stands the American, Thomas Alva Edison (1847 to 1931). He said he could invent anything for anyone. He invented hundreds of useful things. They included the phonograph (or record player) and sticky paper for making parcels.

Like many inventors, Edison made use of other people's ideas. Scientists like Benjamin Franklin, Humphrey Davy and Michael Faraday had made discoveries about electricity. These helped Edison to produce his first important electrical invention. He said he was going to invent a good way of using electricity to provide light. Just over one year later he had invented his light bulb.

Edison knew that things do not burn up without air. He based his light bulb on this fact. He passed an electric current through a thin piece of carbon making sure that there was no air present. The electricity made the carbon glow but it did not burn it up. The hot glowing carbon gave good light.

While Edison was inventing his bulb an Englishman named Joseph Swan made a similar bulb. There were great arguments between the two men about who had made the invention. In 1883 they found a solution and formed the Edison and Swan United Electric Light Company.

# Edison and the light bulb

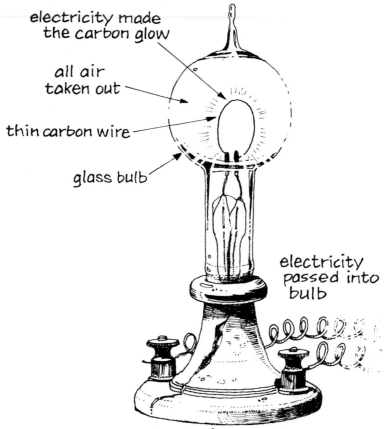

electricity made the carbon glow

all air taken out

thin carbon wire

glass bulb

electricity passed into bulb

EDISON'S LIGHT BULB

The invention of the Edison–Swan bulb was an important step in the story of electric light. However, the story hasn't ended. The bulb has been improved many times. Coloured lamps, for example, were produced to provide a strong, safe light for streets. In the late 1930s the fluorescent tube was invented. The tube is cheaper to run than a bulb. More improvements will come – from more inventors like Thomas Edison.

# Important inventions

For some of these activities you will need to **search** the pages about inventions ( 19 – 26 ).

**1**
  **a**  Why was the wheel and axle an important invention?
  **b**  Why was printing an important invention?
  **c**  Why was the electric light bulb an important invention?

**2**
  Discuss the above inventions with a partner. Decide which you think is the most important invention. Write the result of your discussion and the reasons for your choice.

**3**
  Write **notes** about one difference between each invention when is was first made and as it is now.
Use a chart for your notes.

| INVENTION | AT FIRST | NOW |
|---|---|---|
| Wheel/axle | | |
| printing | | |
| light bulb | | |

**4**
  Write one **fact** and one **opinion** about each of the three inventions – the wheel, printing and the light bulb.

| |
|---|
| **television** |
| **'cat's eye' reflectors** |
| **steam engine** |
| **telephone** |
| **ballpoint pens** |

**5**
  **a**  With a partner choose one of these inventions.
  **b**  Make up three questions about your invention for which you would like to know the answers.
  **c**  Use non-fiction books to help you write an answer for each of your questions.

**FOOTNOTE**

Use the contents page and index in the books to help you find information.

# A map of the world

Use an atlas* or a globe to help you with these activities.

*
You may need to use more than one map to find the information.

**1** Write which of these **continents** each number on the map above stands for. For example ➡ Africa, America (North and South), Antarctica, Asia, Europe, Oceania (Australasia)

    **1  Europe**

**2** **a** Write which of these **oceans** ➡ each letter on the map stands for.
    **b** Why is letter A written in two places on the map?

Arctic Ocean, Atlantic Ocean, Pacific Ocean, Indian Ocean, Southern Ocean

**3** What is the line which is drawn across the middle of the map?

**4** Draw a chart like this:

| AFRICA | AMERICA | ASIA | EUROPE | OCEANIA |
|--------|---------|------|--------|---------|
|        |         |      |        |         |
|        |         |      |        |         |

In the spaces write two countries which are in each continent.

# Venn diagrams

## Read this first

**Venn diagrams** are useful for showing information. They are named after the person who invented them.

Study this Venn diagram carefully to see how it works. It shows which teachers in a school drink tea or coffee at breaktime.

### TEACHERS' DRINKS AT BREAK

These two teachers drink tea but not coffee.

This teacher doesn't drink tea or coffee.

* NOTICE THAT EACH TEACHER'S INITIALS ARE ONLY WRITTEN ONCE.

TEA — HT MV MB

PE AC

COFFEE — KB JC TC CC

These four teachers drink coffee but not tea.

These two teachers drink tea and coffee.

**1**
  **a** What does CC drink?
  **b** What does PE drink?
  **c** What is the total number of teachers who drink tea?

**2** Choose about 15 children and make a Venn diagram to show whether they have sisters or brothers.

**3** Use your diagram to help you write the numbers of children who have
  **a** brothers only;
  **b** sisters;
  **c** both brothers and sisters;
  **d** no brothers or sisters.

**4**
  **a** Draw the Venn diagram below.
  **b** Ask about 15 children if they have a cat, a dog or a fish as pets. Use your diagram to write the number of children who have
  (i) a cat only   (ii) a fish.

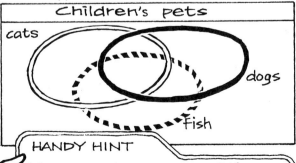

### Children's pets

cats    dogs    fish

HANDY HINT
You must not write any child's initials in more than one space.

# Sorting non-fiction books

## Read this first

Non-fiction books in a library should be sorted into **classes** or **subjects**. This helps you to find books about the subject you are studying.

Some schools and children's libraries put a colour on each book to show which subject it is about. Look at the chart on page 31. The first column shows the colour code used by one school. Each colour stands for a main class or subject.

Many libraries put **Dewey numbers** instead of colours on books to show which subject they are about. Look at the chart again and you will see, for example, that books about religion have numbers between 200 and 299.

**1** Which colour would you look for to find books about
  **a** nursing?
  **b** computers?
  **c** swimming?
  **d** elephants?
  **e** ancient Rome?
  **f** Sahara Desert?

**2** In a library which numbers would you look for to find books about
  **a** science?
  **b** history?
  **c** geography?
  **d** maths?

**3** What main subject would books with these Dewey numbers be about?
  **a** 500   **d** 633
  **b** 450   **e** 792.8
  **c** 915

**4** Use an encyclopedia (or ask your teacher) to help you write a paragraph about the Dewey system for arranging books into subjects.

**5** Explain in writing how the non-fiction books are sorted in your school or class library.

This is the chart used by one school to show how its
**non-fiction books** are sorted:

| Colour code | Dewey number | Main class (or subject) | Some examples to help you |
|---|---|---|---|
| no colour | 000–099 | General reference | **encyclopedias**, year books, etc. |
| | 100–199 | Philosophy | important ideas and beliefs |
| white | 200–299 | Religion | different religions, religious leaders, myths |
| dark blue | 300–399 | Social sciences | police, hospitals, fire service, post office, etc. |
| light blue | 400–499 | Language | **dictionaries**, etc. |
| red | 500–599 | Pure science | animals, plants, chemicals, electricity, etc. (*Note*: mathematics 510–519) |
| yellow | 600–699 | Technology | farming, building, television, computers, etc. |
| black | 700–799 | The arts | music, art, hobbies, sport, dance, drama, etc. |
| orange | 800–899 | Literature | stories, poems |
| green | 900–999 | History, Geography, Biography | **atlases**, countries, people in the past (*Note*: geography 910–919) |

When you first use a library ask the librarian how the books are sorted.

# The life story of our Sun

**1** Write a good **heading** for each of the paragraphs on page 33.

**2** Use the information on page 33 to help you make a **flow chart** showing important stages in the life of the Sun.

**3** Use your flow chart to help you write a paragraph about what will happen to the Sun in the future. Close this book while you are writing the paragraph.

**4** Why do you think all life will cease on Earth if the Sun swells up to become a giant red star? Write your answer and then use non-fiction books to check it.

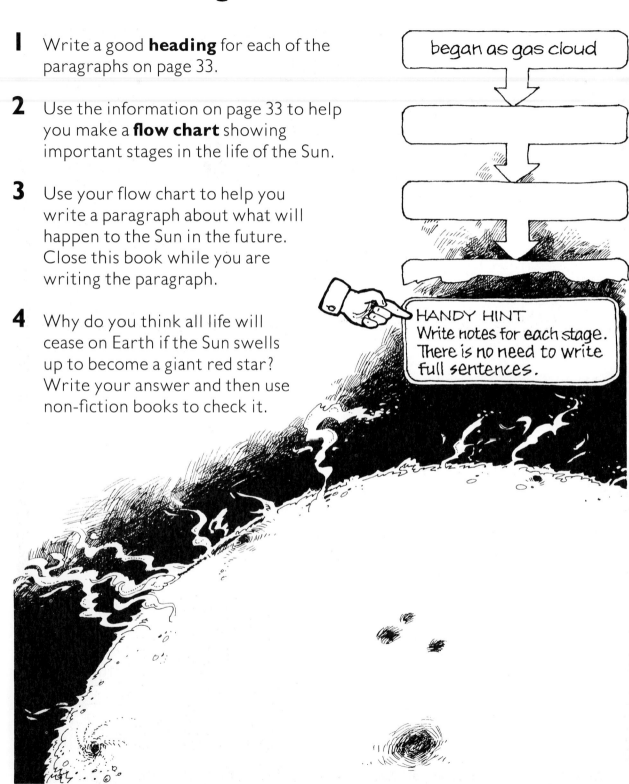

began as gas cloud

HANDY HINT
Write notes for each stage. There is no need to write full sentences.

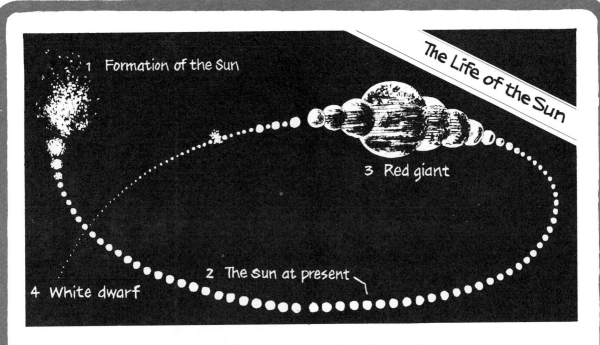

1 Formation of the Sun

3 Red giant

2 The sun at present

4 White dwarf

Astronomers and other scientists believe that the Sun began as a cloud of gas. The middle of the cloud became extremely hot like a giant furnace. The Sun gives out great heat and light and will do this for millions of years into the future.

This is what scientists think will happen in millions of years' time: the gas at the centre of the Sun will be used up. The Sun will get smaller but will then swell up again. It will become a giant red star and all life on Earth will cease. Later the Sun will run out of gas and it will collapse to become a white dwarf star.

Not all stars end their lives in the same way. Stars which are much larger than our Sun end their lives in a huge explosion known as a **supernova**.

# Our Sun and the giant planets

Use the information on pages 35 and 36 to help you with these activities.

**1** Write two reasons why the Sun is the most important object in our solar system.

**2** Write four differences between the Sun and the Earth.

**3** Why do the sunspots look dark?

**4** How does the way the Sun revolves show that it's not solid?

**5** Draw this diagram of the Sun. Label the arrowed parts.

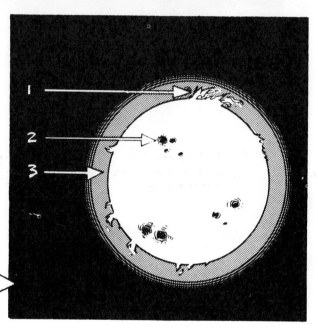

**6** List **four** ways in which Earth and Jupiter are **different** and **four** ways in which they are **similar**.

**7** Write **notes** about Saturn. Use your notes to help you write a paragraph about the planet. Close this book while you are writing the paragraph.

**8** Use non-fiction books to help you write paragraphs about two other planets. (You choose the planets.)

## USE THE STUDY PLAN

**1** Find the book (or books).

**2** Find the information.

**3** Write notes as you read the information.

**4** Close the book (or books).

**5** Use your notes to help you write the paragraph in your own words.

# Our Sun

1  Our Sun is the most important body in our solar system. It is at the centre of the solar system and controls the movements of all the planets. Without its heat and light no living thing could survive on Earth.

2  Our Sun is a star like those we see on a clear night. In fact, many stars are much larger and hotter than our Sun. Our Sun appears larger only because it is the nearest star to the Earth. The Sun is much larger than Earth, however. It is large enough to contain a million Earths.

3  Our Sun doesn't have a solid crust like the Earth. It consists of extremely hot gas – mainly hydrogen. Deep inside the Sun the gas changes and produces nuclear energy. This gives out great heat and light.

4  Like Earth, our Sun revolves but it takes nearly four weeks to revolve once. The poles of the Sun turn more slowly than the rest of the star. This wouldn't happen with a solid body like Earth.

5  Two well-known features of our Sun are the **sunspots** and **prominences**. The sunspots look dark and appear from time to time. They are cooler than the surrounding areas and don't give out as much light. The prominences are like flames coming from the 'surface'. They are hot, bright clouds of gas. Beyond these is a layer of very thin gas called the **corona**.

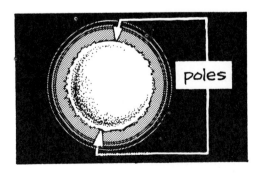

poles

35

# The giant planets

**Jupiter** is the largest planet in our solar system and it has a number of moons. Jupiter is very different from the Earth. It is not a solid body and is made of the gas hydrogen. It gives out about twice as much heat as it receives from the Sun.

Belts of cloud surround Jupiter. The clouds are extremely cold with temperatures much, much colder than ice.

The main feature of Jupiter is perhaps the giant Red Spot which moves around the planet. In 1979 a Voyager spacecraft transmitted pictures of the clouds and showed the Red Spot as a huge whirlpool in the clouds.

**Saturn** is nearly twice as far away from the Earth as Jupiter. It is the other giant planet of our solar system. It also has a number of moons. Like the Sun and Jupiter, it consists largely of the gas hydrogen.

The surface of Saturn is a bit like Jupiter but the clouds are even colder.

The unusual thing about Saturn is its rings. These are separate from the surface of the planet and orbit around its equator. These rings are made up of millions of small particles – some about the size of a brick.

# Sun and Earth

The sentences below need to be sorted. Half of them are mainly about the **Sun** and half mainly about the **Earth.**

**1** Draw two shapes like these:

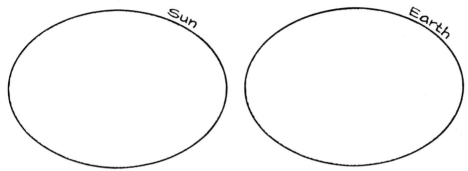

In the first shape write the **numbers** of the sentences which are mainly about the Sun. In the other write the **numbers** of the sentences which are mainly about the Earth.

  **(i)** It is nearly 150 million kilometres away.
 **(ii)** As it travels, it revolves once every 24 hours.
 **(iii)** It is our nearest star.
 **(iv)** This is why we have day and night.
  **(v)** The side which faces the Sun receives its light.
 **(vi)** The Sun is the centre of our solar system.
 **(vii)** It takes Earth $365\frac{1}{4}$ days to travel around the Sun.
**(viii)** It is made of very, very hot gas.
 **(ix)** The side which faces away is in darkness.
  **(x)** This burning gas gives the heat and light we need for life.

**2** Write a paragraph about the Sun using the first group of sentences in the **best order**.

**3** Write a similar paragraph with the second group of sentences.

> **HANDY HINT**
> Work out the order in 'rough' first.

**4** Use the information in your paragraphs to help you draw a diagram showing how we get day and night. Include the Sun and Earth. Label 'night' and 'day' on the Earth.

# Bodies in our solar system

Use the information on pages 39 and 40 to help you with these activities.

**1** The word 'satellite' (or 'satellites') is used three times in the first paragraph on page 39. Read the paragraph and without looking in a dictionary write what you think 'satellite' means. Check your explanation in a dictionary.

**2** Why does the temperature on the Moon change a lot?

**3** What is moonlight?

**4** Why do some meteors burn up while others fall to Earth as meteorites?

**5** Write three ways in which the Moon is
  **a** different from asteroids;
  **b** similar to asteroids.

**6 a** Write three pieces of information from pages 39 and 40 which are about the size of bodies in our solar system.
  **b** Write three pieces of information about the ways the bodies move.

**7 a** Make notes about **asteroids**. Use your notes to help you write a paragraph about asteroids. Make the paragraph as near to 50 words long as you can. Close this book while you are writing the paragraph.
  **b** In the same way write a paragraph about comets which is about 50 words long.

**8** Use your paragraph on comets to help you answer these questions:
  **a** When will Halley's Comet next pass near the Earth?
  **b** How long can a comet's 'tail' be?
  **c** What is different between the paths of comets and planets? (Write two differences.)

## The Moon

Our Moon is the Earth's satellite. It is
unlike the satellites of other planets in
the solar system because it is closer in
size to its 'parent' planet than the other
satellites are. The Moon takes about four
weeks (or a month) to orbit the Earth.
As it moves it keeps the same face towards
the Earth all the time.

The Moon has no atmosphere or water. There is no air to shield it
from the Sun during the long lunar day or to keep its warmth
at night. As a result its temperatures change greatly. The Moon
gives out no light of its own. Moonlight is the Sun's light
reflecting from the Moon's surface.

On the surface of the Moon there are large flat areas. These are
called 'seas' although there is no water on the Moon. There are
craters too. It is thought that some craters were made by
volcanoes and some by meteorites hitting the Moon.

## Asteroids

Asteroids are small solid bodies moving in orbit around the Sun.
Thousands exist. Some are the size of a small rock and some are
about 1000 kilometres in diameter. Asteroids are too small to have
atmospheres and could not have any life on them. They often collide
and pieces sometimes fall to the Earth as meteorites.

Most asteroids orbit the Sun in a belt between Mars and Jupiter.
They are often called **minor planets**.

# Bodies in our solar system

## Meteors and meteorites

**Meteors** are tiny pieces of material which move around the Sun.
Normally they cannot be seen. Sometimes one comes near the Earth
and enters our atmosphere. It rubs against the air and becomes so
hot that it is destroyed in a flash of light. We call this sight
a 'shooting star'. It isn't a star at all.

Some pieces of material from space are large enough to reach the
Earth without being destroyed. These are called **meteorites**. A long
time ago one meteorite made a crater $1\frac{1}{2}$ kilometres wide in the
Arizona Desert. Another in Siberia flattened trees for a hundred
kilometres around.

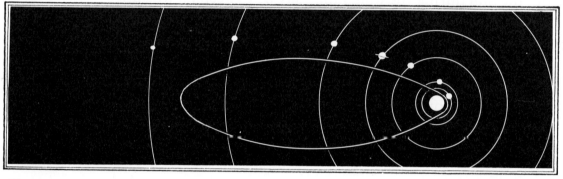

## Comets

Path of Halley's Comet

Comets are very interesting objects which orbit in our solar system.
They have bright 'heads' and long shiny 'tails'. The 'head' is made
of many pieces of material surrounded by thin gas and it could be
as big as Jupiter. The 'tail' can be millions of kilometres long.

Comets pass near the Sun and deep into space. They can take
thousands of years to complete an orbit. Many of them go round the
Sun in the opposite direction to the planets. All of them have their
'tails' pointing away from the Sun as they travel.

Halley's Comet is the best known. It takes about 76 years to
complete its orbit. This brilliant object is visible from Earth
in certain years, and was seen in 1834 and 1910.

# Look into Space

**1** On a large sheet of paper draw this diagram of the bodies in our solar system. Space the diagram out well and number each of the bodies.

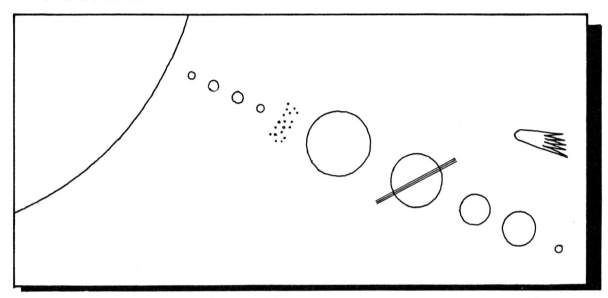

**2** Use the information in this book (pages 32 to 40) and in other non-fiction books to help you complete a chart to go with your diagram. On the chart write

**HANDY HINT**
You will need space for twelve bodies.

**a** the name of each body;
**b** two interesting facts about each body.

| № | Name of body | two interesting **facts** about the body |
|---|---|---|
| 1 | Sun | |
| 2 | Mercury | |
| 3 | | |
| 4 | | |
| 5 | | |
| 6 | | |
| 10 | | |
| 11 | | |
| 12 | Halley's Comet | |

# Book inspection

**1** Choose a topic you would like to know more about – your hobby or special interest perhaps.

**2** Find two non-fiction books which have information about the topic.

**3** Make a chart like the one below for **each** of the two books. Copy the questions in the left-hand spaces. Write your answers in the right-hand spaces. There are instructions to help you.

| | |
|---|---|
| What is the title of the book? | ➡ Write the title. |
| Who wrote the book? | ➡ Write the author's name. |
| Is the book up to date? | ➡ Write the year when the book was published. |
| Is there a contents page? | ➡ Write yes or no. If there is, write the titles of the first and last chapters. |
| Is there an index? | ➡ Write yes or no. If there is, explain how the index shows which pages have pictures/diagrams. |
| Are there any pictures, diagrams, etc.? | ➡ Write yes or no. If the answer is 'yes', write a list of a few of the pictures, diagrams, etc. |
| Are there headings to help the reader? | ➡ Write yes or no. If there are headings, write one or two which you think are important. |

**4** Which of the two books
  **a** has the better pictures or diagrams?
  **b** has the better information?
  **c** do you think is the more useful?
  Write a reason for each answer.

# A glossary

## Read this first

> Some non-fiction books have a **glossary**. It is a kind of dictionary. If a book has a glossary, use it to find the meanings of special and unusual words used in the book.

**1** Search the Contents pages of non-fiction books to help you find two books which have a **glossary**.

**2** Write the following information:
  **a** the author and title of each of the two books;
  **b** in which part of the books the glossary is printed;
  **c** in what order the words are arranged in the glossaries.

**3** Write your own glossary for the section about the **solar system** in this book. Include the meanings of these words:
orbit, moon, planet, star, hydrogen, atmosphere, satellite, solar system.
Start like this:

> GLOSSARY
>
> **atmosphere :** gases which surround a body in space, e.g. Earth.
>
> **hydrogen :**

Use pages 32 to 40 of this book and a dictionary, to help you find the meanings, but don't write any words you don't understand.

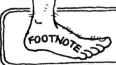 Make a glossary for your next topic or project book.

# Library visit

Visit a library and learn how you can find information about any subject you want to study.

## Before your visit

Read this information carefully:
> The **subject index** in a library is very helpful. It shows the **classification numbers** of the books about each subject. This is part of a subject index.

These are usually Dewey numbers.

| | |
|---|---|
| Space flight | 629.41 |
| Space flight, manned | 629.45 |
| Space research | 500.50 |
| Space shuttles | 629.45 |
| Space stations | 629.44 |
| Space vehicles | 629.4 |
| Space war | 355.02 |

When you go to a library you can search in the subject index for the subject you are studying. Then you can note down the classification numbers for that subject. Next you find the shelves which have books with these numbers. Finally you choose the books you need.

**1** Use the information above to help you make a flow chart showing how you can find books about a particular subject in a library.

## Finding non-fiction books

> 1 Search the . . .

> 2

> 3

> 4

**2** Make an information sheet to complete at the library.
Use these questions to guide you:

**Name of library:**                                    **Date of visit:**

Is there a **subject index**?
Where exactly is it kept?
Is there a catalogue which lists all the books for
each **subject**?
What is this catalogue called?
Is it a card catalogue or is the information on
microfilm (microfiche)?
What information does it give?
In what order is the information?
How can this catalogue help you?

Besides books, are there other resources
(slides, records, etc.) to help you study?
List some if there are.

Take your flow chart and information sheet when you
go to the library.

FINAL HANDY HINT
Always ask the librarian
for help when you need it.

## During your visit

**a** Complete your information sheet.
**b** Choose some subjects that interest you and follow
the steps of your flow chart to find books about them.
Write a short report to explain whether or not your
searches were successful.

FOOTNOTE FOR
THE TEACHER

Try to arrange group visits to a public
library or, if the children are due to
transfer to the next phase of education,
to the library of their future school.

# Using an index: main headings and sub-headings

**1** **a** Copy these eight questions:

(i) What are the prominences on the Sun?

(ii) What caused the craters on our Moon?

(iii) What are Saturn's rings made of?

(iv) What is special about the way the tail of a comet moves?

(v) Where do most asteroids orbit?

(vi) What is the temperature like on Jupiter?

(vii) What happens to a giant red star?

(viii) What is a supernova?

**b** For each question underline in pen the important word you would search for **first** in an index.

**c** Underline in pencil the word you think is **second** in importance. This is the second word you would search for in an index.

## Now read this

> On page 47 is an index for the part of this book which deals with our solar system. For some subjects it has **main headings** and **sub-headings**.

**2** Search the index for the words you underlined above. This will help you to look up the pages and find the information quickly to write an answer for each of the eight questions. Search like this:

1 Use the **most important word** in each sentence to help you find the **main heading** you need.

2 Use the word which is **second in importance** to help you find the **sub-heading** you need.

Now answer the eight questions in **1a**.

# Using an index:

Below is an index for the part of this book which deals with the solar system.

The index has **main headings** ⟶ **asteroids**, 39

and **sub-headings** ⟹ atmosphere, 39

orbit, 39

## Index

# Notes for the teacher

This Study Skills course aims to develop the study skills of readers in primary education. Specific chronological or reading ages are not quoted for the four levels as these are just two factors to be considered when matching the course to the child. The teacher will need to ensure that the child can proceed with **confidence, understanding** and reasonable **independence**.

The course provides a wide range of **skill-building experiences** which contribute towards the development of a **strategy for study**:

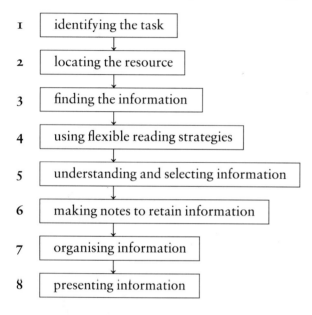

1. identifying the task
2. locating the resource
3. finding the information
4. using flexible reading strategies
5. understanding and selecting information
6. making notes to retain information
7. organising information
8. presenting information

Assignments at each level are grouped into three themes:

| Level 1 | self, family, friends | animals | people at work |
|---------|----------------------|---------|----------------|
| Level 2 | buildings | trees | transport |
| Level 3 | food | communication | explorers |
| Level 4 | problems and solutions | inventions and discoveries | the Solar System |